Touch Your Nose, Wiggle Your Toes

by Mindy Menschell

illustrated
by Jeff Mack

 Harcourt

Orlando   Boston   Dallas   Chicago   San Diego

Visit *The Learning Site!*

www.harcourtschool.com

Do you know your body
parts? Here's a guessing
game to start.

You need it to smell a rose.
Is it your nose?

You need it to carry
your pack.
Is it your back?

You need it to know what
I said.
Is it your head?

You need them to play in
the band.
Are they your hands?

You need them to walk
down the street.
Are they your feet?

You need them to help
you hear.
Are they your ears?

You need them to see
a surprise.
Are they your eyes?

You need them to eat
salty chips.
Are they your lips?

Your body is a wonderful
thing! You need it to do
everything.

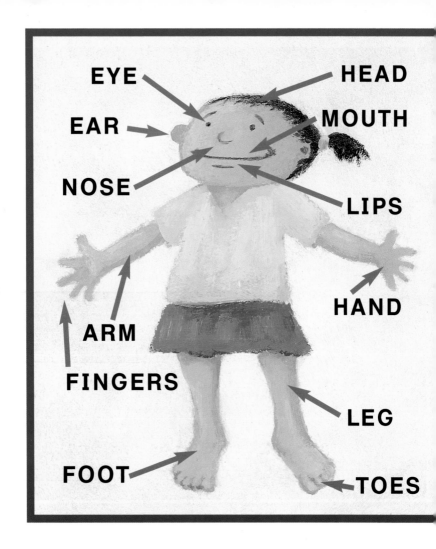

EYE
HEAD
EAR
MOUTH
NOSE
LIPS
HAND
ARM
FINGERS
LEG
FOOT
TOES

You can use this handy
chart. Learn about your
body parts.